The World's Greatest MOM

Herbert I. Kavet

AN Ivory Tower BOOK

CONTEMPORARY
BOOKS, INC.
CHICAGO

To both my moms
who lived too long ago
to exactly fit the example of this book
but who were still the world's greatest moms.

Published by Contemporary Books, Inc.
180 North Michigan Avenue, Chicago, Illinois 60601
Manufactured in the United States of America
International Standard Book Number: 0-8092-5270-8

The World's Greatest MOM

Understood winter fun.

The World's Greatest MOM

Was an expert in making
emergency repairs.

The World's Greatest MOM

Understood when we missed a curfew.

The World's Greatest MOM

Knew which teachers were
best for her kids.

The World's Greatest MOM

Sometimes became too emotionally involved with soaps.

The World's Greatest MOM

Is the world's greatest finder.

The World's Greatest MOM

Evaluated friends with unerring accuracy.

The World's Greatest MOM

Made us feel guilty
when on a diet.

The World's Greatest MOM

Didn't believe in taking chances
with family health.

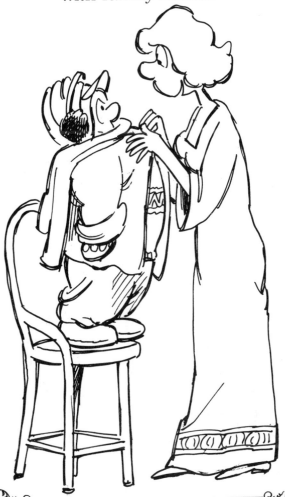

The World's Greatest MOM

Managed the family finances without a computer.

The World's Greatest MOM

Was better than a psychiatrist
when problems arose.

The World's Greatest MOM

Sometimes stretched the truth a little.

The World's Greatest MOM

Knew how to take spots
out of anything.

The World's Greatest MOM

Always loved our favorite films.

The World's Greatest MOM

Taught us proper hygienic care.

The World's Greatest MOM

Explained the benefits
of cleaning my room.

The World's Greatest MOM

Had her own way
of waking us up.

The World's Greatest MOM

Controlled our use of the telephone
so we'd have lots of time for homework.

The World's Greatest MOM

Was the world's best letter writer.

The World's Greatest MOM

Always commanded respect in restaurants.

The World's Greatest MOM

Gave off such a good motherly aroma.

The World's Greatest MOM

Always managed to move through crowds efficiently.

The World's Greatest MOM

Has a great sense of direction.

The World's Greatest MOM

Is still the only infallible person
on Valentine's Day.

The World's Greatest MOM

Remembers everyone's birthday and pretty much knows what everyone wants for a gift.

The World's Greatest MOM

Can replace any six specialists when it comes to dispensing medical advice.

The World's Greatest MOM

Is a wealth of information on family history and remembers every family detail since the beginning of time.

The World's Greatest MOM

Mediated our controversies.

The World's Greatest MOM

Selected the right clothes and sizes for us with unerring accuracy.

The World's Greatest MOM

Always was gracious to our friends.

The World's Greatest MOM

Remembers which vegetables
which kids hate.

The
World's Greatest
MOM

Is the world's best listener.

The World's Greatest MOM

Could discuss sex with us frankly and without embarrassment.

The World's Greatest MOM

Bakes her pies and cakes from scratch.

The World's Greatest MOM

Knows how to keep a secret.

The World's Greatest MOM

Supported her kids' athletic endeavors.

The World's Greatest MOM

Always has enough to eat when the gang drops in.

The World's Greatest MOM

Never refused to car pool her kids anywhere.

The World's Greatest
MOM

Is the only one in the house who knows
how to get the burnt stuff off pots.

The World's Greatest MOM

Could kiss any hurt and make it feel better.

The World's Greatest MOM

Can tell instantly on the phone when something is wrong.

The World's Greatest MOM

Was always patient when waiting for the phone.

The World's Greatest MOM

Was an expert weather forecaster and knew just the right clothes for any combination of inclement weather.

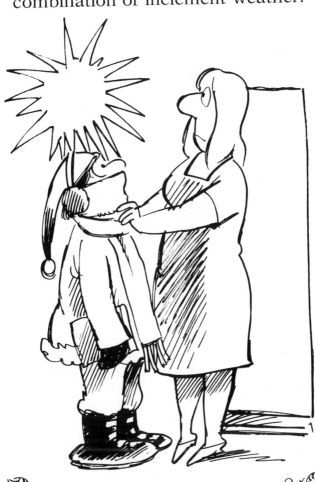

The World's Greatest MOM

Was relaxed about letting me start dating.

The World's Greatest MOM

Can keep a washing machine, refrigerator, or any appliance working with an assortment of paper clips and rubber bands.

The World's Greatest MOM

Is the only family member who can determine whose socks and underwear belong to whom.

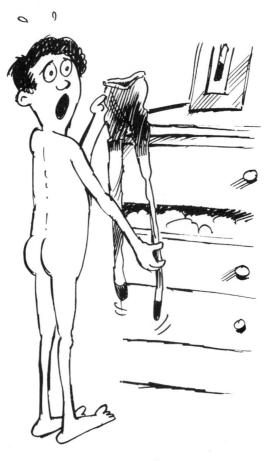

The World's Greatest MOM

Could stay up half the night with a sick baby, car pool the soccer league to a game the next day after work while coping with a major snowstorm, and still have a gourmet dinner ready that evening.

The World's Greatest MOM

Is the only one in the house who can unclog the toilet.

The World's Greatest MOM

Is an expert on romantic problems.

The World's Greatest MOM

Could solve the most difficult "extra question" on homework and could even do math problems.

The World's Greatest MOM

Took over our jobs when we were sick.

The World's Greatest MOM

Let us kids make our own decisions
once we got out on our own.

The World's Greatest MOM

Baited fish hooks for the "brave little kids" and sometimes took the wiggly fish off the hook, and always was willing to clean the fish.

GEORGE'S MARINA

The World's Greatest MOM

Taught us the meaning of courage.

The World's Greatest MOM

Was always willing to type our reports.

The World's Greatest MOM

Learned to live with "our kind of music."

The World's Greatest MOM

Always took an active interest in our hobbies.

The World's Greatest MOM

Always managed that special present for us even if it meant skimping on things she needed.

The World's Greatest MOM

Helps out in financial emergencies.

The World's Greatest MOM

Was always willing to bake for school events that we signed her up for.

The World's Greatest MOM

Never resented our borrowing her clothes (and never borrowed ours).

The World's Greatest MOM

Never complained when I brought laundry home from school.

The World's Greatest MOM

Always ate the parts of the chicken that I didn't like.

The World's Greatest
MOM

Understands the care and feeding of
every plant in existence.

The World's Greatest MOM

Takes care of the pets that I swore
faithfully I would always take care of.

The World's Greatest MOM

Drove me to school on rainy days, or when I was late or had a really bulky project to carry.

The World's Greatest MOM

Supported all my dieting schemes.

The World's Greatest MOM

Always let her children lick the icing off the utensils and bowls.

The World's Greatest MOM

Helped break the news when minor calamities developed.

The World's Greatest MOM

Also makes the world's greatest grandmother.

The World's Greatest
MOM

Gives great advice and still
loves you when you
don't follow it.

The World's Greatest MOM

Could never wait for our birthdays
once she found a present she knew we'd love.

74

The World's Greatest
MOM

Knew the importance of good nutrition.

The World's Greatest MOM

Sent us on wild exotic adventures.

The World's Greatest MOM

Was the hometeam's most reliable supporter.

The World's Greatest MOM

Still had time for love
after working all day.

The World's Greatest MOM

Knows how to deal with overly aggressive sales people.

The World's Greatest
MOM

Can always defuse family disputes.

The World's Greatest MOM

Can solve most emergencies over the telephone.

The World's Greatest MOM

Always compromised on vacations.

The World's Greatest MOM

Was also a second mom to all our good friends.

The World's Greatest
MOM

Interceded with Dad on our behalf.

The World's Greatest MOM

Was indefatigable when we were sick.

The World's Greatest MOM

Was elated over each arts and crafts project.

The World's Greatest MOM

Was and still is my greatest fan.

The World's Greatest
MOM

Knitted the best sweaters.

The World's Greatest MOM

Always cried when
I left for camp.

The World's Greatest MOM

Saw to my cultural enrichment.

The World's Greatest MOM

Protected us in stormy weather.

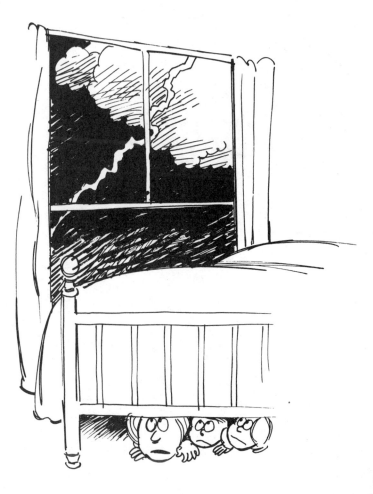

The World's Greatest
MOM

Knows when you really need a hug.

The World's Greatest MOM

Helped furnish my first apartment.

The World's Greatest MOM

Was never embarrassed to
show a little sentiment.

The World's Greatest MOM

Will never have to worry about anyone
taking care of her as long
as her kids are around.

These other humorous titles are available at fine bookstores or by sending $3.95 each plus $1.00 per book to cover postage and handling to the address below.

Please send me:

QUAN.		TITLE
	5352-6	Skinny People Are Dull and Crunchy Like Carrots
	5370-4	A Coloring Book for Pregnant Mothers to Be
	5367-4	Games You Can't Lose
	5358-5	The Trite Report
	5357-7	Happy Birthday Book
	5356-9	Adult Crossword Puzzles
	5359-3	Bridget's Workout Book
	5360-7	Picking Up Girls
	5368-2	Games for the John
	5340-2	Living in Sin
	5341-0	I Love You Even Tho' . . .
	5342-9	You Know You're Over 50 When . . .
	5363-1	You Know You're Over 40 When . .
	5361-5	Wimps
	5354-2	Sex Manual for People Over 30
	5353-4	Small Busted Women Have Big Hearts
	5369-0	Games You Can Play with Your Pussy Cat (and Lots of Other Stuff Cat Owners Should Know)
	5366-6	Calories Don't Count If You Eat Standing Up
	5365-8	Do Diapers Give You Leprosy? What Every Parent Should Know About Bringing Up Babies
	5355-0	I'd Rather Be 40 Than Pregnant
	5362-3	Afterplay: How to Get Rid of Your Partner After Sex

Send me _____ books at $3.95* each $_____

Illinois residents add 8% sales tax; California residents add 6% sales tax: _____

Add $1.00 per book for shipping/handling   _____

                                        TOTAL $_____

☐ Check or M.O. payable to Best Publications
Charge my   ☐ Visa   ☐ MasterCard
Acct. #_____ Exp. Date ____/____
X _____
Signature (required only if charging to Bankcard)
Name _____
Address _____
_____
City/State/Zip _____
*Prices subject to change without notice.
Best Publications, Department IT
180 N. Michigan Ave., Chicago, IL 60601   BB 0784